READING
TEA LEAVES

READING
TEA LEAVES

The Modern Mystic's Guide to
Tea Leaf Divination

A HIGHLAND SEER

Foreword by Leanne Marrama
and Sandra Mariah Wright

ST. MARTIN'S
ESSENTIALS
NEW YORK

Published in the United States by St. Martin's Essentials,
an imprint of St. Martin's Publishing Group

FOREWORD. Copyright © 2022 by Sandra Mariah Wright and Leanne Marrama. All rights
reserved. Printed in the United States of America. For information, address St. Martin's
Publishing Group, 120 Broadway, New York, NY 10271.

www.stmartins.com

Library of Congress Cataloging-in-Publication Data

Names: Highland Seer, author. | Wright, Sandra Mariah, writer of foreword. |
    Marrama, Leanne, writer of foreword.
Title: Reading Tea Leaves : The Modern Mystic's Guide to Tea Leaf
    Divination / A Highland Seer; foreword by Sandra Mariah Wright and Leanne
    Marrama.
Other titles: Tea-Cup Reading and the Art of Fortune-Telling by Tea-Leaves
Description: First St. Martin's Essentials edition. | New York : St. Martin's Essentials,
    [2022] | Series: The Modern Mystic Library; 0 | Previously published as: Reading
    Tea Leaves, 1995.
Identifiers: LCCN 2022013437 | ISBN 9781250803764 (trade paperback) |
    ISBN 9781250803771 (ebook)
Subjects: LCSH: Fortune-telling by tea leaves.
Classification: LCC BF1881 .H54 2022 | DDC 133.3/244—dc23/eng/20220414
LC record available at https://lccn.loc.gov/2022013437

Our books may be purchased in bulk for promotional, educational, or business use.
Please contact your local bookseller or the Macmillan Corporate and
Premium Sales Department at 1-800-221-7945, extension 5442, or
by email at MacmillanSpecialMarkets@macmillan.com.

Reading Tea Leaves was first published as *Tea-Cup Reading and
Fortune-Telling by Tea Leaves* in 1920.

First St. Martin's Essentials Edition: 2022

10 9 8 7 6 5 4 3 2 1

The language of this edition of *Reading Tea Leaves* has been modernized
and updated based on the 1920 edition.

CONTENTS

PUBLISHER'S NOTE

This little book was first written at the beginning of the twentieth century as the world was enduring one brutal war and careening, unknowingly, toward a second. Though the circumstances are vastly different, we find ourselves living through a period of uncertainty and instability that echoes the atmosphere the Highland Seer writes about in the following pages. Today, many people have found themselves looking for answers in places they might have overlooked before—in a deck of tarot cards, in the glint of distant stars, or perhaps in a humble cup of tea. As the Seer notes, during uncertain times we look to new methods "in the hope that some glimmer of light might brighten the darkness and obscurity of the future."

In the face of global strife, whether then or now, reading tea leaves is a quiet, personal practice. This is a fortune-telling tradition that belonged firmly to women. Mothers, sisters, friends, and daughters murmuring together in shared moments, over cups of tea. Dispensing wisdom and seeking advice, commiserating and ranting, celebrating and mourning. And in the midst of a quiet life unfolding in extraordinary times, these women could catch glimpses of the futures they would build in the dregs of their tea.

Reading tea leaves is a practice you can approach however you wish, as a divinatory method, as a gentle way to invite reflection and intuition into your life, or simply as a fun game after the perfect cup of tea. Whatever you choose, brew yourself a fresh cup, settle in, and enjoy *Reading Tea Leaves*.

FOREWORD

If you're reading these words, you've opened a window into the past, and a door to the future. You chose this book, and in doing so, you have set your foot upon the intuitive's path. You may have always known you possessed the gift, or you may be just realizing it now. In either case, your intuition has connected the dots, and you are on your way to strengthening your abilities. We each felt that calling, too, and we believe this knowledge has found its way into the hands of the right people for more than a century.

Leanne writes: *Shortly after the release of* Reading the Leaves, *I had the opportunity to take a shopping adventure at a used bookstore. I believed I had discovered every book available on tea leaf reading until I came across a true gem I had never seen in my local shops. It was a copy of* Reading Tea Leaves *by the Highland Seer. Originally published at the beginning of the twentieth century and hailed as the first book to explore tea leaf reading in the English language, this copy was well worn, a bit shabby—and out of print! I was thrilled to get my hands on this classic that so masterfully covered my favorite form of divination: tea leaf reading, and I immediately called Sandra to share the news of my find. She and I agreed that for its place in history, this book is a must-have reference for all students of tasseomancy (from the French word* tasse, *which means cup, and the Greek word* mancy, *which means divination).*

The mysterious author, credited only as the Highland Seer, clearly shared our view that tea leaf reading is a valuable art of personal divination. Tea leaf reading puts the power of divination into the hands of anyone looking to empower themselves and direct their future. The book contains easy-to-follow instructions for readers to begin practicing the art of tea leaf reading. One of the most important components is a comprehensive list of commonly seen symbols and their traditional meanings; it is oddly comforting to see that people of that time had many of the same concerns we have today, and many of the shapes and their meanings have not changed through the years.

The universe has been nudging us to ask questions from the beginning of time. Nature provides many tools to gain insight, and cultures all over the world have developed and shared these practices through the ages. In Europe, the practice of looking for symbols and images in everyday residues dates to medieval times, when practitioners would melt lead or wax to interpret someone's fate. Even wine sediments and coffee grinds have been consulted, but the queen of all these substances is still tea.

Steeped in enchantment, history, and wonder, tea itself is the subject of myth and legend. According to Chinese lore, tea was discovered almost five thousand years ago. Emperor Shen Nung was resting under a tree when a leaf dropped into his bowl of hot water, and the lovely aroma of the steam enticed him to take a sip. Thus tea as a drink was born. Today, tea is one of the most popular drinks consumed in the world, second only to water.

Mythology aside, anthropologists contend that the tea trees that grow along the lush forested mountains of Yunnan province in China, in Assam in India, in Myanmar (formerly Burma), Laos, Vietnam, and Thailand are descended from the primordial groves where tea originated. From all evidence, tea drinking began here, then spread throughout Asia, making its way from the Far East to the West. Eventually, it became a staple in Scotland.

As for using tea as a means of divination, that can be traced back to the Chinese Ming dynasty (1368–1644 CE), and the advent of the *gaiwan*, a fine porcelain cup suited to the practice of tea leaf reading. The walls of this style of cup fit the recommendations of the Highland Seer, and it is surely the ancestor of the cups the Scots were using by the 1800s when this book was first written: pale and slightly flared, which allows the leaves to cling to them, easily forming dark shapes that would stand out. In the United Kingdom during this time, known as the Victorian Era, the art of tea leaf reading became popular as a method of seeing into the future. The Victorians referred to tea leaf readings as "throwing cups."

It is no surprise that the Victorian Era ushered in an interest in tea leaf reading and divination. This time in history was filled with grief and fear. Even as finely decorated teahouses began popping up all over the country, the world was consumed with plague, and all classes of people wondered what their future would hold. The Victorians could not hide from death. Children often didn't survive past the age of five. Measles, smallpox, whooping cough, and scarlet fever killed the young by the hundreds in many communities. Sicknesses like pneumonia and tuberculosis were common causes of death, and no one was completely safe from their reach.

Today, again we find ourselves wondering what tomorrow will bring. Many people fear the future. It's no surprise to us to find tea leaf reading regaining its popularity in this unsettled global climate. There have been more metaphysical shops and events popping up that advertise tea leaf readings, both in person and online. Near our home base of Salem, Massachusetts, Boston's Tremont Tearoom—opened in 1936—still offers clients wisdom and guidance from information gathered by looking at tea leaves. We have been hosting our own Psychic Tea events in the Commonwealth since 2007, helping our clients get in touch with their intuitive gifts to not only find answers to their questions and concerns but connect them with their loved ones who have passed into spirit. When tea is used as a tool to plan and embrace the future, it heals the soul.

There are countless methods of divination, but what makes tea leaf reading so special is the ease with which it is received. It is approachable for everyone. Many other forms of divination can intimidate the seeker. Tarot cards, runes, bones, and mediumship sometimes frighten people looking for spiritual guidance. Tea offers those who are afraid a more comfortable method of prophecy. *Reading Tea Leaves* by a Highland Seer contains all the information required to begin a practice of tasseomancy. It details the ritual of the reading and provides instruction that can be easily understood and immediately implemented by beginners as well as seasoned psychics looking to learn a new method. While it is written primarily as a guide for those who wish to read for themselves, we maintain that there are many benefits to learning to read for others, too.

Tea brings us to a space where we are united. Tea leaf readings allow us to share in our psychic experience with another person. As Witches, we believe that tea leaf reading is not only a form of divination but also a kind of magick. Tea leaf reading constructs an emotional journey through a person's past, present, and future. As professional psychics, we have found that reading for someone else creates a connection between the reader and the seeker. When people sit down to talk over a cup of tea, the energy of enjoying food and drink creates a bond of intimacy. It is a great tool that helps relax the person seeking guidance. The magick of tea leaf reading encourages seekers and psychics alike to create a special occasion out of the divination practice.

Our advice to you as you embark on this journey is to keep an open mind, especially when you are reading for yourself. Try not to reject a message because it doesn't align with how you believe your future should look. Life has a way of turning out for the best, even if we could never have imagined the road we took to get there. While it can be gratifying to receive confirmation and validation of our desires from the tea leaves, many of the most helpful readings we have given, or received, have been those that highlighted a new perspective, revealed what had been overlooked (or denied), and encouraged a fresh approach to challenges. When a symbol appears that is defined as negative in this book, don't panic. Remember that you have the power to change your future based on the information you receive in your cup. Your destiny resides within your own sphere of influence, and it is not set in stone. The tea leaves provide us with glimpses of what lies ahead, but their true value remains that they give us fair warning, allowing us to manage our own fortune and take charge of our own fate.

Leanne Marrama and Sandra Mariah Wright
Authors of *Reading the Leaves*, *Lighting the Wick*,
and *Awakening the Crystals*
Salem, Massachusetts

PREFACE

It's strange that among all the books published on divination there have been none dealing exclusively with the art of reading tea leaves, even though it is one of the most common forms of divination practiced in Scotland and by local fortune-tellers throughout the country. There might be a brief reference to the teacup method, but in many books it's very clear that the writers are merely acquainted with it by hearsay and haven't studied the art themselves.

This is probably because reading teacups doesn't lend itself to reading the fortunes of naïve seekers for a nice profit. That's one of the reasons tea leaf reading was never adopted by cheap fortune-tellers, who preferred the more obviously lucrative methods of reading palms or tarot cards.

Reading the cup is essentially a domestic form of fortune-telling designed to be practiced at home by anyone willing to take the time to master the simple rules laid down in these pages. This little guidebook was meant to introduce you to the art of reading tea leaves both as a lighthearted pastime around the kitchen table and as the starting point for a more serious study of this fascinating subject.

INTRODUCTION TO THE ART OF TEA LEAF DIVINATION

t's highly likely that there have never been so many people eager to know, to whatever extent is humanly possible, what tomorrow holds as there are at the present moment. The greatest of all wars, which separated so many from those they love and created a deep uncertainty as to what the future might hold, is responsible for this sudden increase in our natural human curiosity about the future. A keen interest in any form of divination is the inevitable result of uncertain times, all in the hope that some glimmer of light might brighten the darkness and obscurity of the future.

Unfortunately, this desperate need for foreknowledge of coming events or information about the well-being of friends and relatives has led to an abundant supply of so-called fortune-tellers who trade on the anxiety and fear of their neighbors and make a living at their expense.

There is an axiom, which centuries of experience demonstrate is as sound as any of Euclid's, that the moment an exchange of money enters into the business of reading the future, the accuracy of the fortune being told disappears. The fortune-teller no longer possesses the singleness of mind or purpose necessary to give a clear reading of the symbols he or she consults. The payment they are receiving is suddenly the first thing on their mind, and this is more than enough to obscure their mental vision and to bias their judgment. This applies to the very highest and most conscientious of fortune-tellers—even those who are truly adept at foreseeing the future when there is no money at stake. The majority of so-called fortune-tellers are charlatans, with only the smallest amount of any actual knowledge of some form of divination: whether by the cards, coins, dice, dominoes, palms, crystal, or any other way. The taint of the money they hope to receive clouds whatever gift or intuition they possess, and so their judgments and prognostications are precisely as valuable as the potions of a quack doctor. They are very different from the Scottish Highlander who stands at the door of his cottage at dawn and carefully notes the signs and omens he observes in the sky, the actions of animals, and the flight of birds, and from them catches a glimpse into the coming events of the day. They differ also from the spae-wife,* who, manipulating the cup from which she's enjoyed her morning tea, looks at the various forms and shapes of the leaves and dregs, and deduces from whom she will receive a letter today; or whether she is likely to go on a journey, or to hear news from across the sea, or to make a nice profit for her goods. In these instances, the taint of money is completely absent. No Highland spae-wife or seer would ever dream of taking a fee for looking into the future on behalf of another person.

If we are equipped with the requisite knowledge and a little skill and intuition, *we* are best able to tell our own fortunes. We cannot pay ourselves for our own prognostications, and without money to taint it, our judgment is unbiased. One of the simplest, most

---

* Scottish term for a fortune-telling woman.

inexpensive, and—as the experience of nearly three centuries has proved—most reliable forms of divination is reading fortunes in teacups. Although it isn't the oldest form of divination, since tea was not introduced to Britain until the middle of the seventeenth century, and for many years was too rare and costly to be used by the majority of the population, the practice of reading the tea leaves doubtless descends from the somewhat similar form of divination known to the Greeks as "κοταβος," which involved divining the future of love by examining the splash made by wine thrown out of a cup into a metal basin. A few spae-wives still practice this method by throwing out the tea leaves into the saucer, but reading the symbols as they are originally formed in the cup is the better method.

After reading this book and following the principles shared here, anyone can quickly learn to read the fortunes that the tea leaves foretell. It's important to understand, however, that teacup fortunes are horary, meaning they deal with events in the coming hours or full day at the most. The immediately forthcoming events cast their shadows, so to speak, within the circle of the cup. The tea leaves can be consulted as

a daily practice and will reveal many of the happenings of daily life, based on the skill and intuition of
the seer. Adepts like the Highland women can and do
foretell events with remarkable accuracy. Practice and
a knowledge of the significance of the various symbols
is all that is necessary in order to become proficient
and to tell your fortune with skill and judgment.

There is, of course, a scientific explanation behind
all the forms of divination practiced. Everyone carries
in themselves their own destiny. Events do not happen to people by chance, but are invariably the result
of some past cause. For instance, a man becomes a
soldier who had never intended to pursue a military
career. This doesn't happen to him by chance, but
because of the prior occurrence of the Great War in
which his country was engaged. The outbreak of war
is similarly the result of other causes, none of which
happened by chance, but were created by still other
occurrences. It is the same with the future. What you
do today happens as a result of something that has
been done in the past, and will, in time, become the
cause of something in the future. The mere act of doing something today sets in motion forces that will
inevitably bring about some entirely unforeseen event.

This event is not decreed by fate or providence, but rather by the person whose actions lead to a future event that she doesn't foresee. In other words, we decree our own destiny and shape our own ends by our actions, whether providence intervenes or not. If this is true, it follows that we carry our destiny within us, and the more powerful our mind and intellect the more clearly this is the case. Therefore, it's possible for a person's mind, formed as the result of past events over which she had no control, to foresee what will occur in the future as the result of deliberate actions. Since only a few people have the ability to see what is about to happen in a vision or by means of the "second sight," the symbols in the tea leaves provide a medium through which to interpret the future. The method or nature of the symbol is unimportant— dice or dominoes, cards or tea leaves. What matters is that the person shaking the dice, shuffling the dominoes, cutting the cards, or turning the teacup is by these very actions transferring the shadows of coming events, all of which have been predetermined by her own actions, from the vague corners of her mind into a new form. Now all that is required is for someone to read and interpret these symbols correctly in order to ascertain what is likely to happen. This is where singleness of purpose and freedom from ulterior motives are necessary in order to avoid error and to form a true and clear judgment.

This is the logical explanation behind the little-understood forms of divination that aim to shed light on the occult. Of all these forms, divination by tea leaves is the simplest, truest, and most easily learned.

Even if the student doesn't deeply believe in the accuracy of what he sees in the cup, reading of the tea leaves is a fun diversion for the breakfast table. The woman who finds a lucky sign such as an anchor or a tree in her cup, or the man who discovers a pair of heart-shaped leaves in conjunction with a ring, will have a little bit of encouragement for their day, even if they only consider the symbols to be harmless superstition.

Regardless of whether the tea leaves are being consulted seriously or as a game, follow the methods in the following chapters carefully and trust that the pictures and symbols formed in your cup are correct.

2

READING TEA LEAVES

The best kind of tea to use for readings is undoubtedly China tea,* the original tea imported to Western nations and still the best for all purposes. Cheaper mixtures contain so much dust and so many fragments of twigs and stems that they are useless for divination, since the tea will not form clear symbols or pictures.

The best shape of cup to employ is one with a wide opening at the top and a bottom that is not too narrow. Cups with almost perpendicular sides are very

---

* The Seer's advice here doesn't necessarily provide a lot of guidance for your next trip to the tea aisle, but many modern tea leaf readers prefer to use gunpowder green tea or another variety of green tea leaf as they unfurl well in the hot water.

difficult to read, because the symbols cannot be seen clearly, and the same is true of small cups. A plain-surfaced breakfast cup is perhaps the best option. The interior should be white and have no pattern printed upon it, as this confuses the clearness of the picture presented by the leaves, as does any fluting or unusual shape.

The ritual of tea leaf reading is very simple. First brew yourself a cup of loose-leaf tea and allow the tea to float freely in the cup, without using a strainer or tea ball. Begin by drinking the contents of your cup, leaving only about half a teaspoon of the liquid remaining with the tea leaves. Take the cup by the handle in your left hand, holding it rim upward, and turn it three times from left to right (clockwise) in one fairly rapid swinging movement. Then very slowly and carefully invert it over the saucer and leave it there for a minute, so all of the tea drains away into the saucer.

If you are approaching the practice seriously, keep your mind focused on your future as you brew and drink the tea and upend the cup. Focus your intention and will on ensuring that the symbols forming under the guidance of your hand and arm (which is of course directed by your brain and thus connected to the future you hold within yourself) correctly represent what is destined for you in the coming day.

The "willing" of the tea is similar to "wishing" when cutting the cards in another time-honored form of fortune-telling. But if you are approaching the leaves as a fun pastime instead of seeking the future in your reading, you can be less intentional in your practice.

Once the tea has drained from the cup, flip it over and you can begin to interpret the meaning of the tea leaves that have remained on the interior of the cup. Hold the cup in one hand and rotate it carefully in order to read the symbols without disturbing them. As long as the remains of the tea have been properly drained away the symbols will remain stable.

The handle of the cup represents the person who is consulting the reading, similar to the "house" in tarot reading. Symbols that are positioned near to the handle are chronologically closer—whether they represent a journey away from home, a message, or visitors to be expected—while symbols that are further from the handle indicate events that are further in some way. This is one of the reasons why reading leaves in the cup, instead of the saucer, is so useful.

The bottom of the cup represents the more remote

future foretold, the events on the sides of the cup are not so far distant, and symbols near the rim indicate occurrences that will happen very soon. The closer the symbols are to the handle in all three cases, the closer they are to being fulfilled. So a symbol found at the rim of the cup right next to the handle will happen imminently, while a symbol at the bottom of the cup opposite the handle will happen furthest in the future.

If the cup has been properly swirled and drained, the tea leaves will be distributed around the bottom and sides of the cup. The fortune can be told equally well regardless of whether there are many leaves or only a few. Of course, there must be some tea leaves in order to create symbols, so the leaves must be allowed to float freely in the tea when it is brewed. There is nothing better than one of the plain old-fashioned earthenware teapots, both for the purpose of preparing a proper cup of tea and for divining the future.

3

GENERAL PRINCIPLES
FOR READING THE CUP

The leaves scattered around the teacup may appear random and accidental, but their arrangement is caused by the movement of the arm when the cup is upended, which is in turn controlled by the mind of the consultant. The scattered leaves will form lines and circles of dots, small clusters, and groups of leaves in patches, all of which will look like a meaningless, random jumble.

Carefully notice all the shapes and figures formed inside the cup. It can be helpful to look at the symbols from different angles to help reveal their meaning. At first it may be difficult to make out what the shapes really are, but as you look at them longer the meaning of each will become clearer. The various symbols in the cup must all be considered together in a general reading. Bad indications will be balanced by good ones; some good ones will be strengthened by others, and so on.

It's now the task of the seer—whether the consultant or another person for whom you are reading—to note what the tea leaves look like. This part of the process is a bit like seeing pictures in the clouds, as children do everywhere. You will see trees, animals, birds, anchors, crowns, coffins, flowers, as well as squares, triangles, and crosses. Each of these possesses, as a symbol, some fortunate or unfortunate significance. The size of each symbol indicates its relative importance. For instance, if you saw a symbol indicating that you would receive an inheritance, if the symbol itself is small you know the inheritance will also be modest, but if the symbol is larger your inheritance will also be significant. If the leaves grouped together form the shape of a crown alongside the symbol for inheritance, you might be led to believe that a title would accompany your inheritance. Chapter 4 contains a list of the meanings of common symbols to help you interpret them.

There are several general principles to know before

you can accurately read the leaves. Isolated leaves or groups of a few leaves or stems frequently form letters or numbers. These letters and numbers should be read in tandem with the other symbols that surround them. If the letter *L* is seen near a small square or oblong leaf, which indicates that the reader will receive a letter or package, it means that the last name of the person who mailed the package begins with *L*. If these two symbols appear near the handle at the rim of the cup, the package will arrive soon; if they appear near the bottom of the cup its delivery will be delayed. If the sign of a letter is accompanied by the appearance of a bird flying toward the "house" (the handle of the cup representing the reader) it means the reader will receive a message; if it is flying away from the house the consultant will be the one sending the message. Birds flying always indicate news of some sort.

Smaller fragments of tea frequently form lines of dots in the cup. These indicate a journey. The length of the line shows the extent of the trip and the direction of the line indicates which direction the reader will be traveling toward. In this case the handle of the cup indicates south. If the consultant is at home and lines lead from the handle around the cup and back to the handle, it shows that they will return. If they end before returning toward the handle it indicates that the consultant will move, particularly if there is a symbol resembling a house near the end of the journey. If the consultant is away from home, lines leading to the handle show a return home. If the line of dots is free from crosses or other symbols of delay, their return trip will be speedy; otherwise it will be postponed. A number may indicate the number of days spent traveling.

A cluster of dots surrounding a symbol always indicate the receipt of money in some form or other, depending on the nature of the symbol. A number positioned near a symbol indicating an inheritance or gift can indicate the amount of the inheritance or the number of gifts to be expected.

You will find that in order to read a fortune with any real accuracy or to read a genuine forecast you cannot be in a hurry. The seer must not only study the general appearance of the horoscope displayed before her and decide what each group of leaves resembles— each of which have a separate significance—but must also balance the bad and the good, the lucky and unlucky symbols, and find a middle ground. For instance, a large bouquet of flowers (a fortunate sign), would outweigh one or two very small crosses (an unfortunate sign), which in this case would merely signify some small delay in the consultant's coming success. In contrast, one large cross in a prominent position would be a warning of disaster that would be hardly, if at all, mitigated by the presence of some small, isolated flowers, regardless of how lucky those signs may be individually. This is the same principle used by astrologers, when, after computing the aspects of the planets toward each other, the Sun and Moon, the ascendant, midheaven, and the significator of the native, they balance the good aspects against the bad, the strong against the weak, the benefics against the malefics, and find an average. In a similar way the lucky and unlucky signs in a teacup must be balanced in order to find the average. Symbols that stand out clearly by themselves have more weight and importance than ones that are hard to discern in the midst of a cloudlike mass of leaves. When these clouds obscure or surround a sign, whether lucky or unlucky, they weaken its force. In teacup reading, however, it is important to remember that the fortune being told is restricted to a single day, unlike in astrology, which deals with the whole life.

If you're only looking for a lighthearted pastime instead of a predicative reading, you can focus solely on the meaning of the symbols and not worry about these more detailed interpretations. In those cases, the seer will just glance at the cup, note the sign for a letter arriving soon, or that for a journey to the coast, or a gift that will soon arrive, or an offer of marriage, and move on to another cup.

You will find that when you examine some cups, they will present no features of interest, or will be so clouded and muddled that you won't be able to find any clear meaning at all. In those cases, the seer shouldn't waste any time over them. Either the consultant has not concentrated his or her attention on the business at hand when turning the cup, or his destiny is so obscured by the indecision of his mind or the vagueness of his ideas that it can't manifest itself through symbols. People who consult the tea leaves too frequently often find this muddled state of things in their cups. Once a week will be often enough to look into the future, although there is something to be said for the Highland custom of examining the leaves from your morning cup of tea in order to catch a glimpse into the events of the day. To "look in the cup" three or four times a day, as some silly people do, is simply to ask for contradictions and confusion, and is often the sign of inactive, empty minds.

The teacup can also be used to ask what is known to astrologers as "a horary question," such as "Will I hear from my lover in France, and when?" In this case the attention of the consultant when turning the cup must be concentrated solely on this single point, and the seer will consider the symbols formed by the tea leaves solely within the context of the question in order to give a definite and satisfactory answer.

AN ALPHABETICAL LIST
OF SYMBOLS AND
THEIR MEANINGS

As you learn to interpret the signs and symbols of the leaves you will soon begin to wonder about the origins of each symbolic meaning. Why does a symbol signify one thing and not something completely different?

The answer, of course, is that the meanings given to the symbols are purely arbitrary, and that there is no scientific reason why one should signify one thing and not another. This is true of all forms of divination. There is no inherent reason why the ace of clubs, for instance, couldn't be considered the "house card" instead of the nine of hearts, or why the double four in dominoes must signify an invitation instead of a wedding, like the double three.

However, if we are attempting to read the future through any kind of symbol—whether it is pips, dots, numbers, or anything else—it's obviously necessary to determine a definite meaning for each symbol before the reading has been cast and to remain faithful to this meaning regardless of the outcome. In the case of tea leaves, where the symbols are not simply based on convention or numbers but are actual shapes and figures like those seen in dreams, the meanings associated with them are the result of long experience. Generations of spae-wives have found that the recurrence of a certain figure in the cup has corresponded with the occurrence of a certain event in the future lives of the various people they have read for. This anecdotal knowledge has been handed down from seer to seer until a tradition of symbols and their meanings has been formed. Based on this tradition we can compile a detailed list of the most important symbols and their meanings. These significations have been organically collected by the writer over many years, chiefly from spae-wives in both Highland and Lowland Scotland, but also in Cornwall, Dartmoor, Middle England, Gloucestershire, and Northumberland. Occasionally one seer attributes a different meaning than another. In these cases, there are several alternative definitions, but because the essence of the symbols is that their meanings are stable and unvarying, the writer has selected whichever meaning is most frequently used or has the best justification for its meaning so that you will not find yourself confused as to how to interpret it.

The following list is in alphabetical order, but there are certain figures and symbols that are so common and have such definite interpretation that it's worth referring to them here specifically. Some of them are signs of approaching good fortune and others of ill fortune.

Common symbols of good fortune are: triangles, stars, trefoil or clover leaves, anchors, trees, garlands and flowers, bridges or arches, and crowns.

The most firmly established symbols of bad fortune are coffins, clouds, crosses, serpents, rats and mice and some other animals, hourglasses, umbrellas, church steeples, swords and guns, ravens, owls, and monkeys.

SYMBOLS AND SIGNIFICATIONS

ABBEY, future ease and freedom from worry.

ACORN, improved health or continued health, strength, and good fortune.

AIRPLANE, unsuccessful projects.

ANCHOR, a lucky sign; success in business and constancy in love; if cloudy, it may mean the reverse.

ANGEL, good news, especially good fortune in love.

ANIMALS, other than those specifically mentioned, foretell misfortune.

APES, secret enemies.

APPLES, long life; prosperity through business.

APPLE TREE, change for the better.

ARCH, a journey abroad.

ARROW, a disagreeable letter coming from the direction the arrow is pointing.

ASS, misfortune overcome by patience; or an inheritance.

AXE, difficulties overcome.

BADGER, long life and prosperity as a bachelor.

BASKET, an addition to the family.

BAT, fruitless journeys or tasks.

BEAR, a long period of travel.

BIRDS, a lucky sign; good news if flying, if at rest a fortunate journey.

BOAT, a friend will visit the consultant.

BOUQUET, one of the luckiest of symbols; loyal friends, success, a happy marriage.

BRIDGE, a favorable journey.

BUILDING, a coming move.

BULL, slander by some enemy or opponent.

BUSH, a social invitation.

BUTTERFLY, success and pleasure.

CAMEL, a burden to be patiently borne.

CANNON, good fortune.

CAR or **CARRIAGE,** approaching wealth; visits from friends.

CART, fluctuations of fortune.

CASTLE, unexpected fortune or an inheritance.

CAT, difficulties caused by treachery.

CATHEDRAL, great prosperity.

CATTLE, prosperity.

CHAIN, an early marriage; if broken, trouble is coming.

CHAIR, an addition to the family.

CHURCH, an inheritance.

CIRCLES, the person whose fortune is read may expect money or gifts.

CLOUDS, serious trouble; if surrounded by dots, financial success.

CLOVER, a very lucky sign; happiness and prosperity. Located at the top of the cup, it will come quickly. As it nears the bottom, it will be increasingly distant.

COCK, much prosperity.

COFFIN, long sickness or sign of the death of a near relation or great friend.

COMET, misfortune and trouble.

COMPASSES, a sign of traveling for work or as a profession.

COW, a prosperous sign.

CROSS, a sign of trouble and delay or even death.

CROWN, success and honor.

CROWN AND CROSS, signifies good fortune resulting from a death.

DAGGER, favors from friends.

DEER, quarrels, disputes; failure in business or commerce.

DOG, a favorable sign; faithful friends if at top of cup; if in the middle of the cup, they are untrustworthy; at the bottom it indicates secret enemies.

DONKEY, a long-awaited inheritance.

DOVE, a lucky symbol; progress in prosperity and affection.

DRAGON, major and sudden changes.

DUCK, increase of wealth by business or commerce.

EAGLE, honor and riches after moving to a new location.

ELEPHANT, a lucky sign; good health.

FALCON, a persistent enemy or competitor.

FERRET, active enemies or competitors.

FISH, good news from abroad; if surrounded by dots, emigration.

FLAG, danger from wounds inflicted by an enemy.

FLEUR-DE-LYS, same as LILY.

FLOWERS, good fortune, success; a happy marriage.

FOX, treachery by a trusted friend.

FROG, success in love and commerce.

GALLOWS, a sign of good luck.

GOAT, a sign of enemies, and of misfortune to a sailor.

GOOSE, happiness; a successful venture.

GRASSHOPPER, a close friend will become a soldier.

GREYHOUND, good fortune brought about by strenuous exertion.

GUN, a sign of discord and slander.

HAMMER, triumph over adversity.

HAND, to be read in conjunction with neighboring symbols and according to whatever it is pointing at.

HARE, a sign of a long journey, or the return of an absent friend. Also of a speedy and fortunate marriage to those who are single.

HARP, marriage; success in love.

HAT, success in life.

HAWK, an enemy.

HEART, pleasures to come; if surrounded by dots, through money; if accompanied by a ring, through marriage.

HEAVENLY BODIES, SUN, MOON, AND STARS, signify happiness and success.

HEN, increase of riches or an addition to the family.

HORSE, desires fulfilled through a prosperous journey.

HORSESHOE, a lucky journey or success in marriage and choosing a partner.

HOURGLASS, imminent peril.

HOUSE, success in business.

HUMAN FIGURES, must be judged according to what they appear to be doing. They are generally good and denote love and marriage.

IVY, honor and happiness through faithful friends.

JACKAL, a sly animal who need not be feared. A mischief-maker of no account.

JOCKEY, successful speculation.

JUG, good health.

KANGAROO, a rival in business or love.

KETTLE, death.

KEY, money, success in business, and a good husband or wife.

KITE, a sign of long travel leading to honor and dignity.

KNIFE, a warning of disaster through quarrels and conflict.

LADDER, a sign of travel.

LEOPARD, a sign of emigration with subsequent success.

LETTERS, shown by square or oblong tea leaves,

signify news. Initials nearby will show the last name of the writers; if accompanied by dots the letter will contain money; if unclouded, the news is good; but if surrounded by clouds, bad news or loss of money.

LILY, at top of cup, health and happiness; a virtuous wife; at bottom, anger and strife.

LINES, journeys and their direction, read in conjunction with other signs of travel; wavy lines denote troublesome journeys or loss suffered en route.

LION, greatness through powerful friends.

LYNX, danger of divorce or the breaking off of an engagement.

MAN, a visitor arriving. If the arm is held out, he brings a present. If the figure is very clear, he is dark-haired; if indistinct, he is blond.

MERMAID, misfortune, especially to seafaring people.

MITER, a sign of honor for a clergyman or through religious agency.

MONKEY, the consultant will be deceived in love.

MOON (as a crescent), prosperity and fortune.

MOUNTAIN, powerful friends; many mountains, equally powerful enemies.

MOUSE, danger of poverty through theft or deception.

MUSHROOM, the sudden separation of lovers after a quarrel.

NUMBERS, depends on symbols in conjunction with them.

OAK, very lucky; long life, good health, profitable business, and a happy marriage.

OBLONG FIGURES, family or business squabbles.

OWL, an evil omen, indicative of sickness, poverty, disgrace, a warning against beginning any new enterprise. If the consultant is in love they will be deceived.

PALM TREE, good luck; success in any undertaking. A sign of children or a speedy marriage.

PARROT, a sign of emigration for a lengthy period.

PEACOCK, denotes success and the acquisition of property; also a happy marriage.

PEAR, great wealth and improved social position;

success in business, and an advantageous marriage.

PEDESTRIAN, good news; an important appointment.

PHEASANT, an inheritance.

PIG, mixed good and bad luck: a faithful lover but envious friends.

PIGEONS, important news if flying; if at rest, domestic bliss and wealth acquired in trade.

PINE TREE, continuous happiness.

PISTOL, disaster.

QUESTION MARK, doubt or disappointment.

RABBIT, fair success in a city or large town.

RAT, treacherous employees; losses through enemies.

RAVEN, death for the aged; disappointment in love, divorce, failure in business, and trouble generally.

RAZOR, lovers' quarrels and separation.

REPTILE, quarrels.

RIDER, good news from overseas regarding financial prospects.

RIFLE, a sign of discord and strife.

RING, a ring means marriage; if a letter is positioned near it in the cup it is the initial of the future spouse. If clouds are near the ring, an unhappy marriage; if all is clear around it, the contrary. A ring right at the bottom of the cup means the wedding will not take place.

ROSE, a lucky sign indicating good fortune and happiness.

SAW, trouble brought about by strangers.

SCALES, a lawsuit.

SCEPTER, a sign of honor from royalty.

SCISSORS, quarrels; illness; separation of lovers.

SERPENT, spiteful enemies; bad luck; illness.

SHARK, danger of death.

SHEEP, success, prosperity.

SHIP, a successful journey.

SNAKES, a sign of bad omen. Great caution is needed to ward off misfortune.

SPIDER, a sign of money coming to the consultant.

SQUARES, comfort and peace.

STAR, a lucky sign; if surrounded by dots it foretells great wealth and honors.

STEEPLE, bad luck.

STRAIGHT LINE, a journey, very pleasant.

STRAIGHT LINES, an indication of peace, happiness, and long life.

SWALLOW, a journey with a pleasant ending.

SWAN, good luck and a happy marriage.

SWORD, dispute, quarrels between lovers; a broken sword, victory of an enemy.

TIMBER, logs of timber indicate business success.

TOAD, deceit and unexpected enemies.

TREES, a lucky sign; a sure indication of prosperity and happiness; surrounded by dots, a fortune in the country.

TRIANGLES, always a sign of good luck and unexpected legacies.

TRIDENT, success and honor in the navy.

TWISTED FIGURES, disturbances and vexation; grievances if there are many figures.

UMBRELLA, annoyance and trouble.

UNICORN, scandal.

VULTURE, bitter foes.

WAGON, a sign of approaching poverty.

WAVY LINES, if long and wavy, they denote loss and trouble. The importance of the lines depends on the number of them and whether they are heavy or light (fewer, lighter lines are less important than a larger number of darker ones).

WHEEL, an inheritance about to fall through.

WINDMILL, success in a new venture or enterprise.

WOLF, beware of jealous intrigues.

WOMAN, pleasure and happiness; if accompanied by dots, wealth or children. Several women indicate scandal.

WOOD, a speedy marriage.

WORMS, secret foes.

YACHT, pleasure and happiness.

YEW TREE, the death of an aged person who will leave their possessions to the consultant.

ZEBRA, travel and adventure in foreign lands.

5

A COLLECTION OF
EXAMPLE CUPS, WITH
INTERPRETATIONS

The following ten figures are copied from actual teacups that have been read and interpreted by real seers. These examples are representative of many different classes of horoscopes, so they are invaluable in showing beginners what symbols to look for and how to discern them clearly as they turn the cup around in their own hands.

Reading the descriptions provided along with each of the illustrations, you will be able to see the principles of interpretation at work. Once you've read and understood the interpretations shared here, you can move on to referencing the alphabetical list of symbols and their meanings in the previous chapter. Between the illustrations and the dictionary of symbols you'll soon be reading proficiently.

INTERPRETATIONS AND ILLUSTRATIONS
INTERPRETATION

This is a fortunate horoscope. The cup shows that the consultant will enjoy success, honor, and wealth in the navy or some maritime-related profession.

The pistols **(A)** on the sides indicate a profession in the military, and the cannon **(B)** in the bottom of the cup along with the trident **(C)** make it clear the consultant will be in the navy. The pear **(D)** on one side and the tree **(E)** on the other are two of the best signs of promotion, rewards, and prosperity. The house **(F)** near the pistol pointing toward the handle of the cup indicates the acquisition of property, but because neither the tree nor the house is surrounded by dots this will be a town, not a country, residence. The repetition of the initial *L* **(G)** may show the name of the admiral, ship, or battle in which the officer will win renown. The triangles (H) confirm the other signs of good fortune.

Principal Symbols—
    Two pistols on sides. (A)
    A cannon in conjunction with a trident in center.
       (B, C)
    A pear. (D)
    A tree. (E)
    A house. (F)
    Initial letters *L*. (G)
    Several small triangles scattered about. (H)

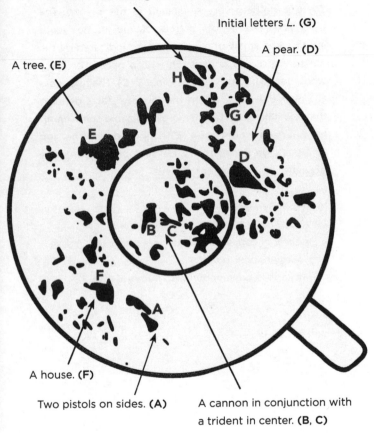

Several small triangles scattered about. **(H)**

Initial letters *L*. **(G)**

A pear. **(D)**

A tree. **(E)**

A house. **(F)**

Two pistols on sides. **(A)**

A cannon in conjunction with a trident in center. **(B, C)**

Figure 1

INTERPRETATION

There is nothing very significant in this teacup. The wavy lines **(A)** denote a troublesome journey leading to some small amount of luck, as indicated by the horseshoe **(B)**, in connection with a person or place whose name begins with the initial *E* **(C)**. The hourglass **(D)** near the place where the journey starts denotes that it will be undertaken in order to avoid some imminent peril. The numeral 4 **(E)** conjoined with the sign of a package shows that a delivery or letter may be expected in that number of days.

Principal Symbols—

    Wavy lines. (A)

    Initial *E* in conjunction with horseshoe. (B, C)

    Hourglass near rim. (D)

    Package in conjunction with numeral 4. (E)

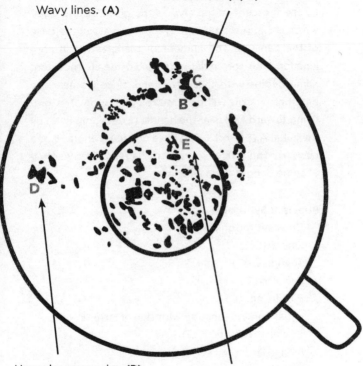

Wavy lines. **(A)**

Initial *E* in conjunction with horseshoe. **(B, C)**

Hourglass near rim. **(D)**

Package in conjunction with numeral 4. **(E)**

Figure 2

INTERPRETATION

This cup predicts prosperity and fortune, indicated by the crescent moon **(A)**, as the result of a journey, which is suggested by the line running along the base of the cup **(B)**. The number of triangles **(C)** in conjunction with the initial *H* **(D)** indicates an important name begins with that letter, and, since it's near the rim, that person will become relevant soon. The bird flying toward and near the handle **(E)**, accompanied by the initial *A* **(F)** and a long envelope **(G)**, denotes good news from an official source. The flag **(H)** gives warning of some danger from an enemy.

Principal Symbols—

Crescent moon. (A)

Line. (B)

Triangles. (C)

Initial *H*. (D)

Bird flying. (E)

Initial *A* in conjunction with sign of letter in official envelope. (F, G)

Flag. (H)

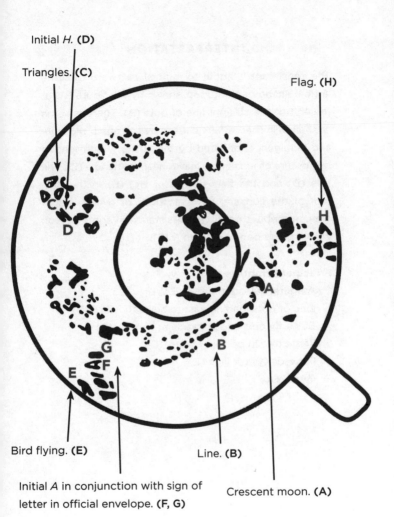

Initial *H*. **(D)**

Triangles. **(C)**

Flag. **(H)**

Bird flying. **(E)**

Line. **(B)**

Initial *A* in conjunction with sign of letter in official envelope. **(F, G)**

Crescent moon. **(A)**

Figure 3

INTERPRETATION

The consultant is about to journey eastward to some large building or institution, shown by the figure **(A)** at the end of the straight line of dots **(B)**. There is some confusion in their affairs caused by too much pleasure and indulgence, denoted by the butterfly surrounded by obscure groups of tea leaves near the handle **(C)**. The tree **(D)** and the fleur-de-lys (or lily) **(E)** in the bottom of the cup are, however, signs of eventual success, probably through the assistance of some person whose name begins with an *N* **(F)**.

Principal Symbols—

    A figure, a head in profile. (A)

    Line of dots leading east to building. (B)

    Butterfly on side approaching handle. (C)

    Large tree in bottom of cup. (D)

    Fleur-de-lys (or lily). (E)

    Initial *N*. (F)

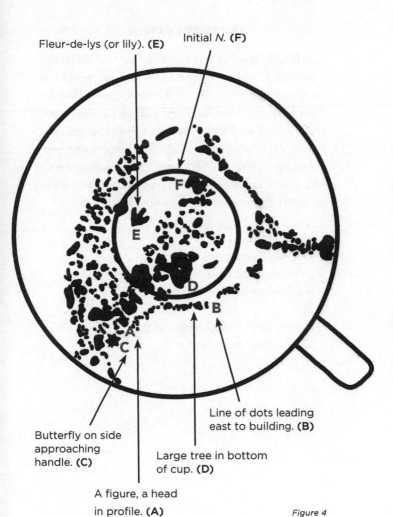

Fleur-de-lys (or lily). **(E)**

Initial *N.* **(F)**

Line of dots leading
east to building. **(B)**

Butterfly on side
approaching
handle. **(C)**

Large tree in bottom
of cup. **(D)**

A figure, a head
in profile. **(A)**

Figure 4

INTERPRETATION

A letter is on its way to the consultant that contains a considerable sum of money, as the symbol for letter is surrounded by dots **(A)**. The future, shown in the bottom of the cup, is not clear, and suggests adversity, but the presence of the hammer **(B)** shows that the consultant will triumph over these obstacles, a sign confirmed by the hat **(C)** on the side. The consultant will be annoyed by somebody whose name begins with *J* and assisted by someone with the initial *Y* **(D)**.

Principal Symbols—

A letter approaching the house,
   surrounded by dots. (A)
Hammer in center of bottom. (B)
Hat. (C)
Initials *J* and *Y* (accompanied
   by small cross). (D)

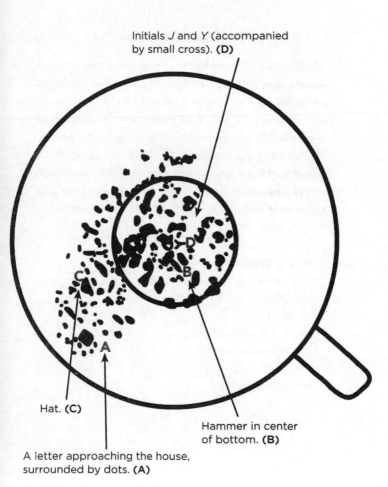

Initials *J* and *Y* (accompanied by small cross). **(D)**

Hat. **(C)**

Hammer in center of bottom. **(B)**

A letter approaching the house, surrounded by dots. **(A)**

Figure 5

INTERPRETATION

A message or letter **(A)** containing good news, shown by bird **(B)** flying and the triangle **(C)**, can be expected immediately. The letter will be received from someone whose initial is *L* **(D)**. If it's from a lover it shows that they are faithful and successful, owing to the anchor **(E)** on the side. The large tree **(F)** on the side of the cup indicates happiness and prosperity. In the bottom of the cup a small cross **(G)** and an initial **(H)** indicate minor vexations or delays in connection with someone whose name begins with *C.*

Principal Symbols—

The letter with the initial *L.* (A, D)
Bird flying high toward handle. (B)
Triangle. (C)
Anchor on side. (E)
Large tree on side. (F)
Small cross. (G)
The initial *C.* (H)

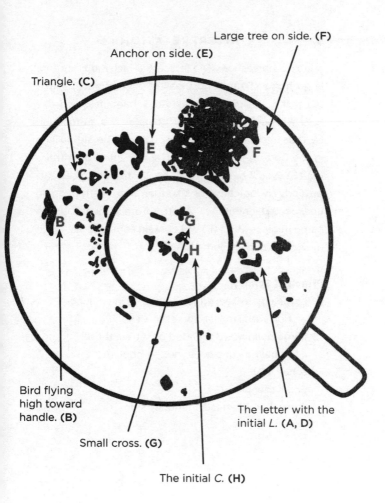

Large tree on side. **(F)**

Anchor on side. **(E)**

Triangle. **(C)**

Bird flying
high toward
handle. **(B)**

The letter with the
initial *L.* **(A, D)**

Small cross. **(G)**

The initial *C.* **(H)**

Figure 6

INTERPRETATION

The two horseshoes **(A)** indicate a lucky journey to a large home **(B)** in a northeasterly direction. The tree **(C)** that is beside it suggests that happiness and fortune will be found there and that (as it is surrounded by dots) it is situated in the country. The sitting hen in the bottom of the cup **(D)**, surmounted by a triangle **(E)** (you'll need to turn the illustration to see this properly) is indicative of a sudden windfall through an unexpected inheritance. A letter from someone whose name begins with T **(F)** will contain some money, but it may not arrive for some time.

Principal Symbols—
Large horseshoe, edge of bottom, in conjunction with smaller horseshoe. (A)
Large building (B) shaded by a tree; these appear as one conjoined symbol. (C)
A hen. (D)
Small triangles. (E)
Initial T with letter and money signs. (F)

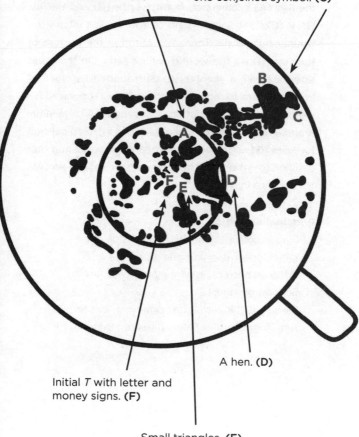

Large horseshoe, edge of bottom, in conjunction with smaller horseshoe. **(A)**

Large building **(B)** shaded by a tree; these appear as one conjoined symbol. **(C)**

A hen. **(D)**

Initial *T* with letter and money signs. **(F)**

Small triangles. **(E)**

Figure 7

INTERPRETATION

This teacup appears to be a warning, as indicated by the flag **(A)** in conjunction with a rifle **(B)** and the letter *V* **(C)**, that some friend of the consultant will be wounded in battle. There is a coffin in the bottom of the cup **(D)**, so the wound will be fatal. On the other side, however, a scepter **(E)**, surrounded by signs of honors, seems to indicate that *V* will be recognized for their bravery by their nation or sovereign. A large initial *K* and a letter sign **(F)** along with the astrological sign for Mars **(G)** underscore this meaning, suggesting that the king (or whomever holds a similar role) will acclaim *V*'s sacrifice in war.

Principal Symbols—

  Flag in conjunction with rifle on side. (A, B)
  Initial *V* near flag and rifle. (C)
  Coffin in bottom, in conjunction with *V.* (D)
  Scepter on side. (E)
  Large initial *K* with letter sign near scepter. (F)
  Astrological sign of Mars between them. (G)

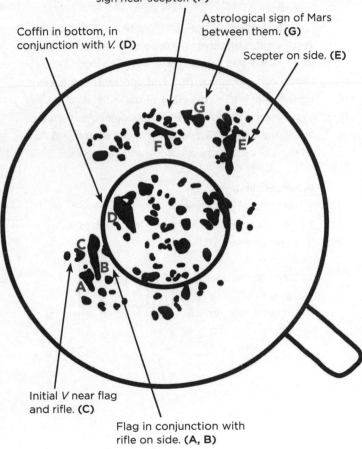

Large initial *K* with letter sign near scepter. **(F)**

Astrological sign of Mars between them. **(G)**

Scepter on side. **(E)**

Coffin in bottom, in conjunction with *V*. **(D)**

Initial *V* near flag and rifle. **(C)**

Flag in conjunction with rifle on side. **(A, B)**

Figure 8

INTERPRETATION

If the consultant is single, the hare **(A)** on the side of the cup indicates that they will soon be married. The figure of a lady holding out an ivy leaf **(B)** is a sign that their sweetheart will prove true and constant. The heart in conjunction with a ring **(C)** and the initial *A* **(D)** points to marriage to a person whose name begins with that letter. The flower **(E)**, triangle **(F)**, and butterfly **(G)** are all signs of prosperity, pleasure, and happiness.

Principal Symbols—

Hare sitting on side. (A)

Figure of woman holding ivy leaf in bottom. (B)

Heart and ring. (C)

Initial *A*. (D)

Large flower on edge of bottom. (E)

Triangle. (F)

Butterfly near rim. (G)

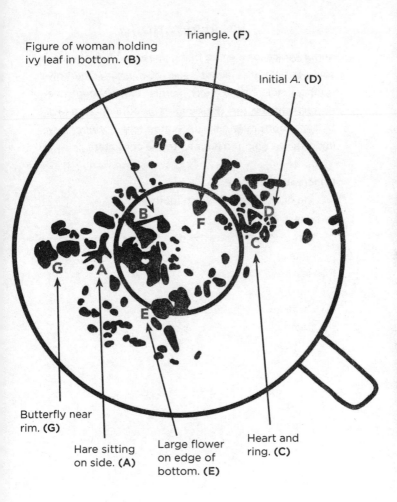

Figure of woman holding ivy leaf in bottom. (B)

Triangle. (F)

Initial *A*. (D)

Butterfly near rim. (G)

Hare sitting on side. (A)

Large flower on edge of bottom. (E)

Heart and ring. (C)

Figure 9

INTERPRETATION

This is typical of the cup being consulted too often by some people. It is almost void of meaning, the only symbols indicating a short journey **(A)**, although the flower near the rim **(B)** denotes good luck. The fact that the bottom is clear indicates that nothing very important is going to happen to the consultant.

Principal Symbols—

Line of dots leading west-southwest. (A)

Flower. (B)

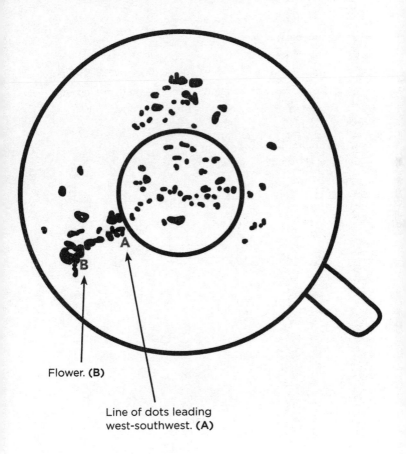

Flower. **(B)**

Line of dots leading
west-southwest. **(A)**

Figure 10

6

OMENS

Omens have long been considered powerful guideposts to the future and can be found in the earliest surviving records of humanity. In the official guide to the British Museum, in the section devoted to Babylonian and Assyrian antiquities (Table case H, Nineveh Gallery), the following appears:

> *By means of omen tablets the Babylonian and Assyrian priests from time immemorial predicted events which they believed would happen in the near or in the remote future. They deduced these omens from the appearance and actions of animals, birds, fish, and reptiles; from*

the appearance of the entrails of sacrificial victims; from the appearance and condition of human and animal offspring at birth; from the state and condition of various members of the human body.

In India, where the records of the early ages of civilization go back hundreds of years, omens are considered of great importance.

Later, in Greece, the home of one of the greatest civilizations, we also find omens regarded very seriously. Today a vast number of intelligent people, all around the world, continue to rely on and respect omens.

It is indisputable that all these thousands of years of history provide good grounds for belief in omens. Whether an omen has been identified as the result of experience—a particular event following close on the heels of the sign being observed—or whether it is an intuitive science, is not quite clear. It seems lazy to dismiss the whole thing as mere superstition, wild guessing, or abject credulity, as some try to do, when the fact remains that omens have, in numberless instances, given good warnings.

To say that these are just coincidences is to beg the question. For the universe is governed by law. Things happen because they must, not simply because they may. There is no such thing as accident or coincidence. We may not be able to see the steps and the connections, but they are there all the same.

In previous times, many signs were deduced from the symptoms of the sick; the events or actions of a person's life; dreams and visions; the appearance of a person's shadow; from fire, flame, light, or smoke; the state and condition of cities and their streets; of fields, marshes, rivers, and lands. From the appearances of the stars and planets, of eclipses, meteors, shooting stars, the direction of winds, the shape of clouds, thunder and lightning and other weather incidents. All these signs and events were able to forecast happenings and countless tablets are devoted to these prophecies.

It's possible that many of these omens arrived in Greece, and it is not unreasonable to believe that India may have derived her knowledge of omens from Babylon; or it may have been the other way about. The greatest of scholars are divided in their opinions as to the origins of this wisdom.

The important point here is that in all parts of the world—even in places where there is no trace of Grecian, Indian, or Babylonian science or civilization—we can still find a system of omens.

This can be explained in two ways. One is that as they grow up, so to speak, all cultures and societies move through the same evolution of ideas and superstitions, which to many modern readers may seem simple or childish. The other explanation seems to be the more reasonable one, if we believe that omens do foretell events: that all peoples and races have accumulated a record, oral or otherwise, of events that have happened and the signs that indicated their occurrence. Over time this knowledge is consolidated and is generally accepted as true. And then it is handed down from generation to generation. Often with the passage of time it gets twisted and a new meaning evolves that is altogether different from the original.

Omens evolved in various ways over time. In Greece sneezing was a good omen and was considered a proof of the truth of what the sneezer had just said. A tingling in the hand denoted that money would soon fill that hand; a ringing in the ears that news will soon be received. The number of sneezes later came to have particular meanings. The hand that tingled, either right or left, indicated whether money would be paid or received. The particular ear affected was thought to indicate good or bad news. Other involuntary movements of the body were also considered of prime importance.

Many omens are derived from the observation of various substances dropped into a bowl of water. In Babylon oil was used. Today in various countries melted lead, wax, or an egg white are all commonly used. In many European folk practices, the shapes that result could indicate the trade or occupation of a future spouse, the luck for the year, and so on. Finns use stearine and melted lead; Magyars use lead; Russians use wax; Danes use lead and egg; and the northern counties of England use egg, wax, and oil.

Bird omens were the subject of very serious study in Greece. It has been thought that this was because in the early mythology of Greece some of their gods and goddesses were believed to have been birds. Thus, birds were particularly sacred, and their appearances and movements were of profound significance. The principal birds used for signs were the raven, crow, heron, wren, dove, woodpecker, and kingfisher, and all the birds of prey such as the hawk, eagle, or vulture, which the ancients classed together, as per W. R. Halliday, in his book, *Greek Divination*. Many curious instances of accurate bird omens are related in *The Other World*, by Reverend Frederick Lee.

"In the ancient family of Ferrers, of Chartley Park, in Staffordshire, a herd of wild cattle is preserved. A tradition arose in the time of Henry III that the birth of a parti-coloured calf is a sure omen of death, within the same year, to a member of the Lord Ferrers family. By a noticeable coincidence, a calf of this description has been born whenever a death has happened of late years in this noble family." (*Staffordshire Chronicle*, July 1835).

Similarly if a picture or statue of an individual falls from its place, this is usually regarded as an evil omen. Many cases are cited where someone has died soon after their likeness has fallen.

It would be easy to multiply examples of this kind of personal omen. The history and traditions of many old families in England are saturated with it. The predictions and omens relating to certain well-known families recur repeatedly. We can infer that beneath the common beliefs and superstitions there is enough fire and truth to justify the smoke, and to justify the faith placed in the modern books on omens and dreams.

Classifying omens can prove difficult. Many books have been written on the subject and there are more yet to be written on the meaning of omens in various cultures. In this book you'll find a collection of common omens from various sources.

OMENS

ACORN—Falling from the oak tree and hitting someone, is a sign of good fortune to the person it strikes.

BAT—To see one during the day means a long journey.

BIRTHDAYS—

"Monday's child is fair of face,
Tuesday's child is full of grace,
Wednesday's child is full of woe,
Thursday's child has far to go,
Friday's child is loving and giving,
Saturday's child works hard for its living;
But a child that's born on the Sabbath-day

Is handsome and wise and loving and gay."

BUTTERFLY—In your room it indicates great pleasure and success, but you must not catch it, or the luck will change.

CANDLE—A spark on the wick of a candle means a letter or message for the person who first sees it. A large glow like a parcel means money is coming to you.

CAT—If a black cat comes to your house, it means difficulties caused by treachery. Chase it away and avoid trouble.

CHAIN—If your necklace breaks while you are wearing it, it means disappointment or a broken engagement.

CLOTHES—To put on clothes inside-out is a sign of good luck, but you must leave them on that way or the luck will change.

CLOVER—To find a four-leaf clover means luck, happiness, and prosperity.

COW—If a cow comes into your yard or garden it is a very prosperous sign.

CRICKETS—A lucky omen. They foretell money coming to you. They should not be disturbed.

DEATH-WATCH BEETLE—A clicking in the wall by this little insect is regarded as evil, but it does not necessarily mean a death; possibly only sickness.

DOG—Coming to your house, it means faithful friends and is a favorable sign.

EARS—You are being talked about if your ear tingles. Some say, "Right for spite, left for love." Others reverse this omen. If you think of the person, friend, or acquaintance who is likely talking about you, and mention the name aloud, the tingling will stop if you say the right one.

FLAG—If it falls from the staff while flying, it means someone will be wounded by an enemy.

FRUIT STONES OR PIPS—Think of a wish first, and then count your stones or pips. If the number is even, the omen is good. If odd, the reverse is the case.

GRASSHOPPER—In the house means an important friend or distinguished person will visit you.

HORSESHOE—To find one will bring you luck.

KNIVES—Crossed are a bad omen. If a knife or fork falls to the ground and sticks in the floor you will have a visitor.

LADYBUGS—A sign that a visitor is coming.

LOOKING GLASS—Breaking one will bring you ill luck.

MAGPIES—One, bad luck; two, good luck; three, a wedding; four, a birth.

MARRIAGE—Sunshine and a cat sneezing are both good luck for a wedding.

MAY—"Marry in May, and you'll rue the day."

NEW MOON—On a Monday, it signifies good luck and good weather. If you see a new moon for the first time by looking over your right shoulder it is a chance for a wish to come true.

NIGHTINGALE—Lucky for lovers if heard before the cuckoo.

OWLS—Evil omens. Continuous hooting of owls in your trees is thought to be a sign of sickness or poor health.

PIGS—To meet a sow coming toward you is good; but if she turns away, the luck does too.

RABBITS—A rabbit running across your path is said to be unlucky.

RAT—A rat running in front of you means treacherous servants and loss through theft.

RAVEN—To see one means death to the elderly and trouble in general.

SALT—Spilled salt means a quarrel. This may be avoided by throwing a pinch over the left shoulder.

SCISSORS—If they fall and stick in the floor it means quarrels, illness, or the breakup of lovers.

SERPENT OR SNAKE—If it crosses your path, it means spiteful enemies and bad luck. Kill it and your luck will be reversed.

SHOES—The right shoe is the best one to put on first.

SHOOTING STARS—If you wish, while the star is still moving, your wish will come true.

SINGING—Before breakfast, you'll cry before night.

SPIDERS—The little red spider is the money spider, and means good fortune coming to you. It must not be disturbed. Long-legged spiders are also signs of good fortune.

TOWEL—To wipe your hands on a towel at the same time as someone else, means you will quarrel with them in the near future.

WHEEL—The wheel coming off any vehicle you are riding in means you will receive an inheritance; it's a good omen.

WASHING HANDS—If you wash your hands in the water just used by someone else, you can expect a quarrel unless you make the sign of the cross over the water first.

NOTES

Date: _____

Question or Intention: _____

_____

_____

_____

_____

_____

_____

Symbols and Locations: _____

_____

_____

_____

_____

_____

_____

Interpretation: _____

_____

_____

_____

_____

Date: _____

Question or Intention: _____
_____
_____
_____
_____
_____

Symbols and Locations: _____
_____
_____
_____
_____
_____

Interpretation: _____
_____
_____
_____
_____

A HIGHLAND SEER

Date: _____

Question or Intention: _____
_____
_____
_____
_____
_____
_____

Symbols and Locations: _____
_____
_____
_____
_____
_____
_____

Interpretation: _____
_____
_____
_____
_____

Date: _____

Question or Intention: _____
_____
_____
_____
_____
_____
_____

Symbols and Locations: _____
_____
_____
_____
_____
_____
_____

Interpretation: _____
_____
_____
_____
_____

Date: _____

Question or Intention: _____

_____

_____

_____

_____

_____

Symbols and Locations: _____

_____

_____

_____

_____

_____

Interpretation: _____

_____

_____

_____

_____

Date: _____

Question or Intention: _____
_____
_____
_____
_____
_____
_____

Symbols and Locations: _____
_____
_____
_____
_____
_____
_____

Interpretation: _____
_____
_____
_____
_____

Date: _____

Question or Intention: _____
_____
_____
_____
_____
_____

Symbols and Locations: _____
_____
_____
_____
_____
_____

Interpretation: _____
_____
_____
_____
_____

Date: _____

Question or Intention: _____
_____
_____
_____
_____
_____
_____

Symbols and Locations: _____
_____
_____
_____
_____
_____
_____

Interpretation: _____
_____
_____
_____
_____

ABOUT THE AUTHORS

Reading Tea Leaves was published in 1920 by the unnamed "Highland Seer." Though their book continues to live on, the seer's identity has been long forgotten.

Leanne Marrama is a full-time psychic medium at the shop she co-owns, Pentagram Witchcraft & Magick Shoppe in Salem, Massachusetts. She teaches classes and presents at festivals around the country. Marrama is the coauthor of *Reading the Leaves, Lighting the Wick,* and *Awakening the Crystals*. She has been featured on TLC's *What Not to Wear, Ghost Chronicles,* and *Beyond Belief with George Noory,* among many other media appearances.

Sandra Mariah Wright is the High Priestess of Elphame Coven in Salem, Massachusetts. She teaches workshops and offers her witchy wares at festivals, including her own, Spirit Beacon Psychic Fair and

Mystical Marketplace. Her occult supply company, Gallows Hill Witchery, was the first to host live crystal sales online via social media. Wright is the coauthor of *Reading the Leaves, Lighting the Wick,* and *Awakening the Crystals,* and hosts a monthly radio show with Leanne Marrama called *The Psychic Tea,* which is simultaneously broadcast and archived on their Facebook page. She has appeared on the Travel Channel, Showtime, and *The Real Housewives of New York City.*